"If therefore the light that is in thee be darkness, how great is that darkness!"

Matthew 6:23

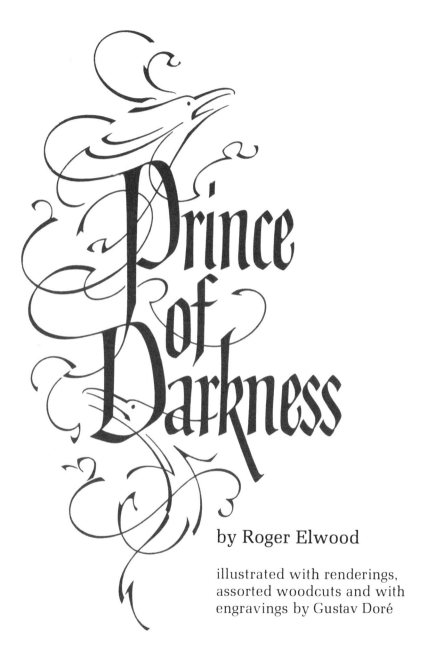

by Roger Elwood

illustrated with renderings,
assorted woodcuts and with
engravings by Gustav Doré

Published by The C. R. Gibson Company,
Norwalk, Connecticut.

CONTENTS

THE FALL OF THE REBEL ANGELS

The Origin of Satan

CHAPTER I

Where did Satan come from? Was he always considered "the Prince of Darkness"?

It may come as a surprise that Satan once occupied a very high place in heaven and shone as a being of great beauty. An indication of just how impressive Satan was may be gained from Ezekiel 28: 13-15 wherein the Lord refers to the former glory of the King of Tyre.

"Thou hast been in Eden the garden of God; every precious stone was thy covering, the sardius, topaz, and the diamond, the beryl, the onyx, and the jasper, the sapphire, the emerald, and the carbuncle, and gold: the workmanship of thy tabrets and of thy pipes was prepared in thee in the day that thou wast created. Thou art the anointed cherub that covereth; and I have set thee so: thou wast upon the holy mountain of God; thou hast walked up and down in the midst of the stones of fire. Thou wast perfect in thy ways from the day that thou wast created, till iniquity was found in thee."

This was something of the "station in life" that Satan enjoyed in God's presence. But for Satan, something was lacking! How many people seem to have everything—personal magnetism, considerable influence, quite a bit of money, and are not satisfied?

BEAUTY LED TO VANITY—AND WORSE

It was undoubtedly his splendor and high station that goaded Satan to rebellion, harboring thoughts of grandeur and deluding himself into believing that he could make himself equal to or, even, superior to his Creator.

As Isaiah 14:12-14 points out, "How art thou fallen from heaven, O Lucifer, son of the morning! how art thou cut down to the ground, which didst weaken the nations! For thou has said in thine heart, I will ascend into heaven, I will exalt my throne above the stars of God: ... I will ascend above the heights of the clouds; I will be like the most High."

1 Timothy 3:6 underlines this, " ... lest being lifted up with pride he fall into the condemnation of the devil." In other words, Satan fell under the condemnation of God as a result of pride that drove him to decidedly unholy ambition.

THE DISRUPTOR OF HEAVEN

Though Adam and Eve were the first to sin among human beings, Satan was the first sinner in the angelic realm. 1 John 3:8 establishes this fact, "He that committeth sin is of the devil; for the devil sinneth from the beginning."

That the break between Satan and God was anything but a "clean" one is shown by Revelation 12:7-9, "And there was war in heaven: Michael and his angels fought against the dragon; and the dragon fought and his angels." And here is what happened, "And prevailed not; neither was their place found any more in heaven. And the

great dragon was cast out, that old serpent, called the Devil, and Satan, which deceiveth the whole world: he was cast out into the earth, and his angels were cast out with him." Jesus personally describes Satan's fall from heaven in Luke 10:18, "And he said unto them, I beheld Satan as lightning fall from heaven".

Satan was not the only rebel, the leader, yes, the organizer, but one of many who joined together in this "war in heaven." These followers of Satan are the demons spoken of throughout Scripture.

II Peter 2:4 refers to them as "the angels that sinned." Jude 6 describes them as "the angels which kept not their first estate, but left their own habitation." They choose to follow Satan, a conscious, deliberate act on their part which sealed their ultimate doom.

FROM HEAVEN TO—

The fall of Satan is dealt with symbolically in Revelation 12:4, "And his tail drew the third part of the stars of heaven, and did cast them to the earth." The tail is that of the dragon, Satan, and it may be that fully a third of all the angels in Heaven joined him. As *Ellicott's Bible Commentary* states, "The stars are the light-bearers ... who were given high place by God that they might be burning and shining lights for Him. A large proportion of these are drawn away in the train of evil. They are dragged down from the height of the grandest possibilities of good to the low level of an existence enslaved to evil."

John Milton, in *Paradise Lost,* dealt with the fall of Satan in this brief excerpt,

"But O how fallen! how changed
From him, who in the happy realms of light,
Clothed with transcendent brightness didst outshine
Myriads though bright."

We can see that Satan and his fallen angels were once favored with God's glory, they were beautiful, and outwardly praiseworthy creations. But, as we also are told, "Pride goeth before destruction, and an haughty spirit before a fall." (Proverbs 16:18) And their pride precipitated ages of tribulation.

It is through these verses that we can understand more about the origin of Satan. The Bible has not provided an overabundance of information, yet enough to assure us that Satan had every gift from God, but chose to go his own way, asserting an independence with disastrous consequences. Just what these consequences are will become clearer in the following chapters.

SATAN APPROACHING EARTH

His Reality and Appearance

CHAPTER II

Satan has been portrayed in a variety of guises, television programs have presented him as a sophisticated charmer who seems to be a combination of Casanova, the Count of Monte Cristo and other such real or fictional characters, and motion pictures have frequently contributed to this conception. A notable exception is *The Exorcist* which presents the reality of Satan in terrifyingly evil terms. But during centuries gone by, Satan was accorded a grotesque, animal-like appearance.

St. Anthony claimed that Satan manifested himself as a pig-faced creature, and such artists as Goya, Bosch and Giotto favored the billygoat version. According to one report, to these artists Satan was both goat and human in form, having at all times the horns, the legs and the beard of a goat, often the torso of a human being and often with wings.

Different races view Satan in wildly disparate forms. Among the California Indians he is called Coyote, in northern Siberia he is the Great Crow. Other races see Satan as a snake, a bat, even a raging volcano erupting with lava at times of great anger! The stereotyped Christian view of Satan in the Garden of Eden may well be a highly inappropriate one, at least according to today's conception of serpent. As Dr. Merrill Unger indicates in *Unger's Bible Handbook,* "The Edenic serpent (Satan's agent) was not a writhing serpent, which was the result of God's curse, but doubtless the most cunning and beautiful of God's animal creatures." In other words, Satan did not become the serpent but spoke through this creature. At the time it was a stunning creature indeed, perhaps as beautiful in its way as, say, the bird of paradise is today. Dr. Unger further points out that Genesis 3:14 gives an often overlooked revelation about the serpent, "And the Lord God said unto the serpent, Because thou hast done this, thou art cursed above all cattle, and above every beast of the field; upon thy belly shalt thou go, and dust shalt thou eat all the days of thy life." Before Adam's fall, the serpent did not crawl upon its belly and was not cursed above all creatures. God was determined that the serpent would never again be used by Satan and would become a symbol of man's fall from absolute communion with his Creator.

RELIGIOUS CONTROVERSY

Some theologians deny that Satan is an actual person, and some deny his existence altogether. They claim that such ideas belong to the Dark Ages of fear and superstition—and do not have any place in today's scientific era of increasing enlightenment.

I Timothy 4:1 anticipates this view with a prediction, "Now the Spirit speaketh expressly, that in the latter times some shall depart from the faith, giving heed to seducing spirits, and doctrines of devils".

In January 1974, the spiritual leader of some 65 million Anglicans, the Archbishop of Canterbury, The Most Reverend Arthur Michael Ramsey, said, "I believe there is genuine demonaic possession and a genuine exorcism".

But belief in a personal devil is clearly evident in a 1973 statement made by Pope Paul VI. Here, in part, is what he said, "We know that this dark and disturbing Spirit really exists, and that he still acts with treacherous cunning, he is the secret enemy that sows errors and misfortunes in human history ... He is the treacherous and cunning enchanter ... "

WHAT THE BIBLE TELLS

The Bible presents the reality of Satan in many passages. For example, Job 1:6 states, "Now there was a day when the sons of God came to present themselves before the Lord, and Satan came also among them". There is no indication that this verse is meant to be taken allegorically. Satan came—and that is a biblical assertion of fact.

Other portions of Scripture reinforce the reality of Satan. One of the best-known involves Christ's wilderness temptation. Matthew 4:1 declares, "Then was Jesus led up of the spirit into the wilderness to be tempted of the devil." This is presented as a personal confrontation between Christ and Satan. In verse 5, we are told, "Then the devil taketh him up into the holy city, and setteth him on a pinnacle of the temple." And, in verse 8: "Again, the devil taketh him up into an exceeding high mountain, and sheweth him all the kingdoms of the world . . . "

The New Testament is abundant with other verses which depict Satan's reality.

WORLD-WIDE DECEPTION

The personality of Satan as viewed by man has changed over the years. Where once there was fear, there is now either skepticism and denial or outright, flagrant worship.

Poet Alfred J. Hough expressed it well:

> "Men don't believe in a devil now,
> As their fathers used to do,
> They've forced the door of the broadest creed
> To let his majesty through,
> There isn't a print on his cloven foot,
> Or a fiery dart from his bow,
> To be found in earth or air to-day,
> For the world has voted so.
>
> "But who is mixing the fatal draft
> That palsies heart and brain,
> And loads the earth of each passing year
> With ten hundred thousand slain?
> Who blights the bloom of the land to-day
> With the fiery breath of hell,
> If the devil isn't and never was?
> Won't somebody rise and tell?"

FIRST APPROACH OF THE SERPENT IN EDEN

His Character

CHAPTER III

A ROARING ADVERSARY

The Bible has plenty to say about the character and the personality of Satan. I Peter 5:8 warns, "Be sober, be vigilant; because your adversary the devil, as a roaring lion, walketh about, seeking whom he may devour."

As an adversary, Satan is as ferocious as a lion on the rampage. And the lion is not called "King of Beasts" without reason.

Even stronger terms are offered by John 8:44, "Ye are of your father the devil, and the lusts of your father ye will do. He was a murderer from the beginning, and abode not in the truth, because there is no truth in him. When he speaketh a lie, he speaketh of his own: for he is a liar, and the father of it."

Satan is called a murderer, a liar and one with a whole catalogue of "lusts." And this verse suggests that anyone who lies is being influenced by Satan because he was, in the Garden of Eden, the father of lies.

II Corinthians 4:4 refers to Satan as the god of this world who "hath blinded the minds of them which believe not ... " He is someone who is constantly attacking unbelievers, trying to prevent them from gaining spiritual truth.

The children of disobedience are those who refuse to pay allegiance to God. And according to Ephesians 2:2, the prince of the power of the air has great control over such individuals. "The prince of the power of the air" is another name given to Satan.

Satan apparently promotes spiritual darkness whenever and wherever he can. Colossians 1:13 calls him "the power of darkness." Without Satan, there would be no spiritual darkness—for he is the power behind this darkness.

THE GUISES OF SATAN

Journalist Edward M. Bounds wrote, "He (the devil) wears disguises, but his ends are single and lie in only one direction, double-faced but never double-minded, never undecided, never vague or feeble in his purposes or ends. No irresolution, nor hesitant depression nor aimless action spring from him. The devil has character if not horns, for character is often harder and sharper than horns. Character is felt. We feel the devil. He orders things, controls things. He is a great manager. He manages bad men, often good men and bad angels. Indirect, sinister, low and worldly is the devil as a manager."

Satan is subtle, devious. Genesis 3:1 states, "Now the serpent was more subtil than any beast of the field." This verse serves two purposes; it gives us another name for Satan (the serpent) and it also mentions that one aspect of his character is subtlety. II Corinthians 11:3 reinforces this statement, "But I fear, lest by any means, as the serpent beguiled Eve through his subtilty, so your minds should be corrupted from the simplicity that is in Christ."

That man's mind should sometimes be deceived is small wonder, for Satan's wiles are varied. "And no marvel; for Satan himself is transformed into an angel of light." (II Corinthians 11:14)

THE NAMES OF SATAN

Satan is known by many names in the Bible. We find him named Adversary in I Peter 5:8 Deceiver of the whole world in Revelations 12:9, Murderer and liar in John 8:44, and Lucifer, in Isaiah 14:12, but the most frequent name is Satan which is found with nearly as much frequency in the Old Testament as in the New Testament.

However, references to Satan uncover him in a host of guises. Here are just a few:

1. Crooked serpent (Isaiah 27:1)
2. Dragon (Isaiah 27:1, Revelation 20:2)
3. Piercing serpent (Isaiah 27:1)
4. Prince of the devils (Matthew 12:24)
5. Tempter (Matthew 4:3, 1 Thessalonians 3:5)
6. The god of this world (II Corinthians 4:4)
7. Unclean spirit (Matthew 12:43)
8. Wicked one (Matthew 13:19, 38)

THE GREAT TEMPTER

That Satan tempts is obvious from even a cursory reading of the Bible. Here are just a few illustrative verses, "Defraud ye not one the other, except it be with consent for a time, that ye may give yourselves to fasting and prayer; and come together again, that Satan tempt you not for your incontinency." (I Corinthians 7:5). "For this cause, when I could no longer forbear, I sent to know your faith, lest by some means the tempter have tempted you, and our labour be in vain." (I Thessalonians 3:5). "For some are already turned aside after Satan." (I Timothy 5:15).

The Book of Job is especially fruitful in giving us insight to Satan's character. The first chapter tells us how he was permitted to tempt Job. "And the Lord said unto Satan, Hast thou considered my servant Job, that there is none like him in the earth, a perfect and an upright

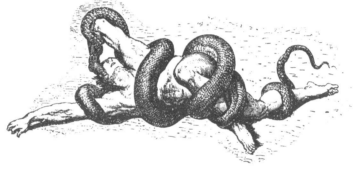

man, one that feareth God, and escheweth evil? Then Satan answered the Lord, and said, Doth Job fear God for nought? Hast not thou made an hedge about him, and about his house, and about all that he hath on every side? thou hast blessed the work of his hands, and his substance is increased in the land. But put forth thine hand now, and touch all that he hath, and he will curse thee to thy face. And the Lord said unto Satan, Behold, all that he hath is in thy power; only upon himself put not forth thine hand. So Satan went forth from the presence of the Lord". (Job I 8:12).

At the Last Supper, it was Satan who tempted Judas as reported in John 13:2, "And supper being ended, the devil having now put into the heart of Judas Iscariot, Simon's son, to betray him."

In view of all this testimony from Scripture, it is obvious why Satan, the tempter, is also called the Enemy—for verse after verse portrays him as an opponent in the spiritual battles of life.

THE LAST SUPPER

SATAN IN COUNCIL

His Power and Domain

CHAPTER IV

Where does Satan operate? What has the Bible to say about his domain or kingdom?

II Corinthians 4:4 sheds some light on the answers to these questions, "In whom the god of this world hath blinded the minds of them which believe not . . . "

The god of this world.
Not Christ. Nor the Almighty.
But Satan.

THE GOD OF THIS WORLD

"And the Lord said unto Satan, Whence comest thou? Then Satan answered the Lord, and said, From going to and fro in the earth, and from walking up and down in it". (Job 1:7)

Revelations 12:12 tells in no uncertain terms about Satan's presence on earth, "Therefore rejoice, ye heavens, and ye that dwell in them. Woe to the inhabiters of the earth and of the sea! for the devil is come down unto you, having great wrath, because he knoweth that he hath but a short time".

But though Satan's time is limited, "the prince of this world" (John 12:31) has great power while it lasts.

AN EVIL DRAMA

How does Satan use his power in the world? We know he is the leading character in an evil drama wherein the souls of men are cast in sinful roles. Satan is the paramount influence, the creator of all the misery and suffering in this domain. With the aid of his demons, he creates anguish and suffering in scattered parts of the globe.

In his *Histoire admirable de la possession et conversion d'une penitente* (1613) Father Michaélis lists three hierarchies of demons; (1) Belzebuth, Leviathan, Asmodeus, Balberith, Astaroth, Verrin, Gresil, Sonnillon; (2) Carreau, Carnivean, Oeillet, Rosier, Verrier; and (3) Belial, Olivier, Juvart. He ascribes to these demons the following attributes: Belzebuth tempts through pride; Leviathan tempts one's faith; Asmodeus tempts through luxury; Balberith suggests blasphemy and homicide; Astaroth tempts through vanity or laziness; Verrin through impatience; Gresil through impurity; Sonnillon through hatred; Carreau tempts without pity; Carnivean

tempts through obscenity; Oeillet tempts against poverty; Rosier tempts through love; Verrier tempts against obedience; Belial tempts through arrogance; Olivier through cruelty and avarice; and Juvart takes control of different bodies.

The sinful nature of every human being on the face of the earth gives him easy entrance. Psalms: 109:6 tells us that Satan personifies wickedness, "Set thou a wicked man over him: and let Satan stand at his right hand".

I John 5:18-19 is a reference to Satan: "We know that whosoever is born of God sinneth not; but he that is begotten of God keepeth himself, and that wicked one toucheth him not. And we know that we are of God, and the whole world lieth in wickedness."

In other words, "The whole world is in the hands of the Prince of Darkness: Satan."

Ephesians 6:12 reinforces this view, "For we wrestle not against flesh and blood, but against principalities, against powers, against the rulers of the darkness of this world, against spiritual wickedness in high places."

"Principalities and powers" is a reference to not only the heads of government who conduct the affairs of state wickedly but, also, to the demoniac influences which propel them. This is true of "the rulers of the darkness of this world," which can be considered a reference to demons as well as the men and women who are instrumental in fostering this darkness. "Darkness" primarily means spiritual darkness or separation from God.

HEAVEN—PARADISE LOST

That Satan has communication with heaven is obvious from Job and other passages which show that Satan accused Job before God; and that he also was in contention with Michael the archangel (over the body of Moses). But having communication with heaven does not mean that heaven should be considered, in any way, part of Satan's domain. The significant point is that Satan's influence is not felt in heaven, and hasn't been since his fall from God's kingdom; he can control, as it were, only on earth. However, God through the Holy Spirit exercises control in Satan's kingdom—which illustrates that Satan's power is limited while God's is not.

HELL—A PLACE OF TORMENT

And there is another aspect of Satan's domain. This world, we have established, is one region, the other is hell. Several Greek and

Hebrew words used in the Old and New Testaments depict hell, each with a slightly different connotation. But while they both agree that hell is a place of terrible anguish, the main differences in interpretation lie in when unbelievers are to be sent there, directly after death or at the Day of Judgment.

Another phrase used to depict hell in the Bible is "the bottomless pit." And Satan is described, in Revelation 9:11, as "the angel of the bottomless pit, whose name in the Hebrew tongue is Abaddon, but in the Greek tongue . . . Apollyon."

A PITILESS DEVIL—A COMPASSIONATE GOD

It is not difficult to picture in our minds the form of Satan flitting between hell and this earth, counting the souls in hell, laughing with fiendish glee as he sees another soul lost on earth and heading for torment. And likewise, one has no difficulty imagining Jesus seeing all of this and weeping, as He did from time to time while He lived on earth in human form. The reason is the same in each instance, the sinfulness of human nature, a weakness which thrills its exploiter, the Prince of Darkness.

The Bible offers many verses dealing with this condition. For example, "For there is no faithfulness in their mouth; their inward part is very wickedness; their throat is an open sepulchre; they flatter with their tongue." (Psalm 5:9)

And even stronger is the statement in Psalm 14:1-3, "The fool hath said in his heart, There is no God. They are corrupt, they have done abominable works, there is none that doeth good. The Lord looked down from heaven upon the children of men, to see if there were any that did understand, and seek God. They are all gone aside, they are all together become filthy: there is none that doeth good, no, not one."

And, of course, Isaiah 64:6 is further confirmation, "We are all as an unclean thing, and all our righteousnesses are as filthy rags; and we all do fade as a leaf; and our iniquities, like the wind have taken us away."

And Satan rejoices at all this!

SATAN'S POWER

Satan is not all-powerful. But he is powerful enough to cause terrible turmoil and suffering in the world, as he has done in the past, is doing right now and will continue to do in the future.

Not even the highest of angels can really prevail against him, "Yet Michael the archangel, when contending with the devil he disputed about the body of Moses, durst not bring against him a railing accusation, but said, The Lord rebuke thee." (Jude:9)

It was not Michael who was able to rebuke Satan, but God through Michael who did so. The archangel had not sufficient power of his own to deal with Satan.

Ephesians 2:2-3 vividly depicts several of the manifestations of Satan's power, the results of his unholy influence, "Wherein in time past ye walked according to the course of this world, according to the prince of the power of the air, the spirit that now worketh in the children of disobedience: Among whom also we all had our conversation in times past in the lusts of our flesh, fulfilling the desires of the flesh and of the mind; and were by nature the children of wrath, even as others."

Unbelievers are shown to be instruments of Satan here, and in and through them he brings forth abundant fruit, in the form of fleshly lusts and indulgence in them. Psalm 106:36-38 adds, "And they served their idols: which were a snare unto them. Yea, they sacrificed their sons and their daughters unto devils, And shed innocent blood, even the blood of their sons and of their daughters, whom they sacrificed unto the idols of Canaan and the land was polluted with blood ... " And Revelation 9:21 concludes, "Neither repented they of their murders, nor of their sorceries, nor of their fornication, nor of their thefts."

THE BODY—BUT NOT THE SOUL

The book of Job provides a graphic picture of how severely Satan can afflict even God's children. He could cause the death of loved ones, business reverses and allied disasters, physical disease and suffering, mental anguish and other tribulations, but he could not touch Job's soul—this holy man was one of God's own and his soul was protected by the Almighty. "For I know that my redeemer liveth, and that he shall stand at the latter day upon the earth: And though after my skin worms destroy this body, yet in my flesh shall I see God." (Job 19:25-26). Ultimately, of course, Job had in store a better life than before, for God rewarded him for the faith that was able to sustain him through the worst of Satan's afflictions.

UNFERTILE GROUND

Mark 4:15, in relating the conclusion of Christ's parable about the sower, states, "And these are they by the way side, where the word is sown; but when they have heard, Satan cometh immediately, and taketh away the word that was sown in their hearts."

Some people hear the Word of God and, in effect, it goes in one ear and out the other. They receive it casually and do not heed its message. In the long run, it is as though they had never heard a single verse to begin with. According to Mark 4:15, Satan is behind this non-receptivity.

THE DEMON OF PRIDE

Satan uses pride to cause the downfall of many human beings. Paul wrote, in I Timothy 3:6-7: " . . . lest being lifted up with pride he fall into the condemnation of the devil. Morever he must have a good report of them which are without; lest he fall into reproach and the snare of the devil."

Pride here is meant in the sense of egotism, that self-aggrandizing sort of pride that causes a man or a woman to think of himself or herself as being better than the next person. It is a pride that neglects modesty and leads to unkindness and an uncharitable attitude toward others.

The Bible has scores of admonitions against pride, emphasizing how dangerous pride can be when used as a weapon of Satan. Luke 1:51 is typical, " . . . he hath scattered the proud in the imagination of their hearts." But one of the most outspoken is Psalm 73:6, 8-9, "Pride compasseth them about as a chain; violence covereth them as a garment. They are corrupt, and speak wickedly concerning oppression: they speak loftily. They set their mouth against the heavens, and their tongue walketh through the earth."

Pride and vanity are both well known to Satan and together, are a combination powerful enough to bring down any foolish man.

MASTER OF DECEPTION

We read earlier that Satan has the ability to transform himself into an angel of light. (II Corinthians 11:14) And his ministers (demons) can also pose as ministers of righteousness (verse 15). This means that his power is such that he is able to motivate even pious men. Their outward appearance is appropriately faithful, even their conduct and words carry the veneer of true belief—but beneath all this they are really agents of the Prince of Darkness, marionettes with Satan himself the master puppeteer controlling the strings.

This power of Satan to deceive is perhaps one of his most potent because from it can stem a host of sins, sexual immorality, murder, robbery and other transgressions. As John 8:44 states, "Ye are of your father the devil, and the lusts of your father ye will do."

1 John 2:16-17 brings this point even more sharply home, "For all that is in the world, the lust of the flesh, and the lust of the eyes, and the pride of life, is not of the Father, but is of the world. And the world passeth away, and the lust thereof: but he that doeth the will of God abideth for ever."

FALLEN ANGELS ON THE WING

His Purpose

CHAPTER V

All of the implications of Satan's manuever-
ings can be summarized in one sentence: His
purpose is to frustrate the will of God. Whatev-
er God's purpose, you can be sure that Satan
is automatically opposed to it. When human
beings seek to be led by God, Satan is bound
to place obstacles in the way, to thwart any
connection, as it were, between creation and
Creator. According to Alfred Edersheim, in *The
Life and Times of Jesus the Messiah*, Satan,
"having in vain tried to prevent the creation
of man, at last conspired to lead him into sin
as ... the means of his ruin—the task being
undertaken by Sammael (another name for
Satan) and his angels. The instrument employed
was the serpent ... "

Job 9:24 states, "The earth is given into the
hand of the wicked: he covereth the faces of
the judges thereof." A somewhat better transla-
tion of the first part of this verse would be,
"The earth is given into the hand of the wicked
one." Some men whose job should be to in-
terpret law with justice, to rule in God—given
wisdom are often blinded by Satan and foster
instead a host of injustices.

AN EVIL REAPER OF MEN'S SOULS

Christ's dealings with Simon Peter give us a further clarification of the overall purpose of Satan.

"And the Lord said, Simon, Simon, behold, Satan hath desired to have you, that he may sift you as wheat." (Luke 22:31) Satan wanted to subvert even one of the apostles, one of the men who walked daily with Christ. John 6:70-71 tells how he succeeded, "Jesus answered them, Have not I chosen you twelve, and one of you is a devil? He spake of Judas Iscariot the son of Simon: for he it was that should betray him, being one of the twelve." The stereotyped depiction of Death as the Grim Reaper is really a better representation of Satan than most, because death can be either a release unto God or unto the Devil, and if it is the latter, it couldn't be any more grim!

To serve Satan's purpose he must keep men and women in darkness, the spiritual darkness of separation from Almighty God. II Corinthians 4:4 confirms this: "In whom the god of this world hath blinded the minds of them which believe not, lest the light of the glorious gospel of Christ, who is the image of God, should shine unto them". Jesus tells of God's purpose in Acts 26:18, "To open their eyes, and to turn them from darkness to light, and from the power of Satan unto God, that they may receive forgiveness of sins, and inheritance among them which are sanctified by faith that is in me."

Thus, it is clear that God's purpose is to open men's eyes, while Satan's is to close them, God's purpose is to bring man forgiveness of sins, while Satan's purpose is to guarantee everlasting condemnation for those sins.

CHILDLIKE FAITH

We are told in Scripture that faith must be childlike, that it must be simple and unquestioning and all-encompassing in nature. "Therefore being justified by faith, we have peace with God through our Lord Jesus Christ." (Romans 5:1). According to II Corinthians 11:3, Satan corrupted Eve from the simplicity of her original communion with God.

Whenever worship becomes so ritualized and elaborate that the form of worship assumes more importance than the purpose—which is to glorify God—Satan has once again managed to exert his influence. This was a primary reason behind the direction taken by St. Francis of Assisi, he wanted to get back to the basic teachings of Christ. He disavowed all material things and became a beggar, wandering the streets and preaching humility and God's love.

A WRECKER OF GOVERNMENTS—A TORMENTOR OF INDIVIDUALS

Satan held sway with Hitler, Mussolini, Stalin, and with other tyrants throughout the ages. Satan triumphed in and through these men. "Having spoiled principalities and powers, he made a shew of them openly, triumphing over them ... " (Colossians 2:15) He dominated them, he paraded them around on the world stage, he set them to committing atrocities, and he glorified in their acts, gloated over the maimed and the dying left in their wake. As the English divine, Thomas Adams, wrote, "The devil is no idle spirit, but a vagrant, runagate walker, that never rests in one place. The motive, cause and main intention of his walking is to ruin man." When man, God's creation, is ruined by the devil, this frustrates the will of God who made man in his own image. An anonymous quotation, written two centuries ago, reinforces this thought: "Talk of devils being confined to hell, or hidden by invisibility! We have them by shoals in the crowded towns and cities of the world. Talk of raising the devil! What need for that, when he is constantly walking to and fro in our streets, seeking whom he may devour."

Satan will seldom let even believers rest. He will do all within his power to get them to turn from God. Such a devoted disciple as Paul experienced this sort of onslaught. As he states in II Corinthians 12:7, "And lest I should be exalted above measure through the abundance of the revelations, there was given to me a thorn in the flesh, the messenger of Satan to buffet me, lest I should be exalted above measure."

In the repetition of those seven words . . . "lest I should be exalted above measure," God seems to be trying to tell us, through Paul, that even in our spiritual growth there can be pitfalls, hence, Satanic danger, in that we might come to pursue such growth for personal egotism and not for closer communion with God.

A FALSE WORSHIP

An axiomatic part of Satan's program for the human race is to cause worship to be directed toward himself. He seeks to blind the minds of men away from God, and to "open" those minds fully to him. He is determined to supplant God whenever, wherever and however he can. Today we are witness to such manifestations as Satan worship, weird religious cults and so forth. Susy Smith, author of Today's Witches, argues there are today 60,000 witches in the United States alone! And these come about as a result of spirits manipulated by Satan to seduce the unwary. Acts 13:8-10 cites an example, "But Elymas the sorcerer (for so is his name by interpretation) withstood them, seeking to turn away the deputy from the faith. Then Saul, (who also is called Paul,) filled with the Holy Ghost, set his eyes on him, And said, O full of all subtilty and all mischief, thou child of the devil, thou enemy of all righteousness, wilt thou not cease to pervert the right ways of the Lord?"

The Bible gives other examples of sorcery such as the magicians who could duplicate many (but not all) of the God-given feats of Moses and Aaron.

"Then Pharoah also called the wise men and the sorcerers: now the magicians of Egypt, they also did in like manner with their enchantments. For they cast down every man his rod, and they became serpents: but Aaron's rod swallowed up their rods." Exodus 7:11-12

Again in Exodus 8:6-7 "And Aaron stretched out his hand over the waters of Egypt; and the frogs came up, and covered the land of Egypt. And the magicians did so with their enchantments, and brought up frogs upon the land of Egypt".

A certain man called Simon deceived the people of Samaria with sorcery in the Acts 8:9-11 account. "But there was a certain man, called Simon, which beforetime in the same city used sorcery, and bewitched the people of Samaria, giving out that himself was some great one: To whom they all gave heed, from the least to the greatest, saying, This man is the great power of God. And to him they had regard, because that of long time he had bewitched them with sorceries".

Deuteronomy 18:10-12 tells us of those things which are abominations to God. "There shall not be found among you any one that maketh his son or his daughter to pass through the fire, or that useth divination, or an observer of times, or an enchanter, or a witch, Or a charmer, or a consulter with familiar spirits, or a wizard or a necromancer. For all that do these things are an abomination unto the Lord: and because of these abominations the Lord thy God doth drive them out from before thee". To those who worship anything but God, I Corinthians 10:20-21 says, "But I say, that the things which the Gentiles sacrifice, they sacrifice to devils, and not to God: and I would not that ye should have fellowship with devils. Ye cannot drink the cup of the Lord, and the cup of devils: ye cannot be partakers of the Lord's table, and of the table of devils." To those who look to Satan for anything less than evil, Jesus tells us in Mark 3:23,26 "And he called them unto him, and said unto them in parables, How can Satan cast out Satan? And if Satan rise up against himself, and be divided, he cannot stand, but hath an end."

There can be no doubt—based upon the ample evidence offered by God's Word—that false worship is wicked, as Satan himself is wicked, and that he will stop at nothing to see his purposes fulfilled. "Those by the way side are they that hear; then cometh the devil, and taketh away the word out of their hearts, lest they should believe and be saved." (Luke 8:12). "The field is the world; the good seed are the children of the kingdom; but the tares are the children of the wicked one; The enemy that sowed them is the devil; the harvest is the end of the world; and the reapers are the angels." (Matthew 13:38-39).

DANCE OF SATAN

FIRE BY SORCERY

JESUS EXORCISING A DEVIL

Christ and Satan

CHAPTER VI:

Whenever Christ did confront Satan—directly or through Satan's demons—the inevitable result was victory for the Son of God. He had but to speak a few words or touch the afflicted one with His hands, and thus it was that good literally triumphed over evil.

THE WILDERNESS ENCOUNTER

Christ was tempted by Satan during a forty-day period in the wilderness. According to some theologians, this period was a miniature of the forty years spent by the Irsraelites in the wilderness after their liberation from the Egyptians. Christ as a single entity bore all the temptations that were faced by hundreds of thousands of God's Chosen People many centuries before. The difference was that the Israelites succumbed while Christ did not.

This singular assumption by Christ of the experiences of many was a thread that ran through to Calvary where He bore the sins of the entire human race on the Cross; thus, in tempting Christ during that wilderness time, Satan was really trying to cause the *downfall* of the human race. If Christ could be seduced, then every human being would be helpless before the devil's on-slaught. That Christ was consistently victorious is a biblical depiction of how believers can be victorious over the tempter.

Satan's appeals to Christ fell into the following categories: [1] Satisfaction of physical appetite; [2] An attack against spiritual trust; [3] The lust of the eyes.

DIVINE REBUKE

First, Satan tempted Christ in the matter of satisfaction of physical appetite. According to Matthew 4:2-11, "And when he had fasted forty days and forty nights, he was afterward an hungred. And when the tempter came to him, he said, If thou be the Son of God, command that these stones be made bread."

This was an attempt by Satan to get Christ to demonstrate His incarnate deity. In other words, if Christ were really God in the flesh, then Christ had unlimited power at His disposal. And that power—which could heal the sick, still the tempest at sea, enable Him to walk on water—surely could cause ordinary stones and pebbles to be transformed into edible bread.

Christ's reply was unequivocal: "It is written, Man shall not live by bread alone, but by every word that proceedeth out of the mouth of God."

Spiritual trust was assaulted next.

"Then the devil taketh him up into the holy city, and setteth him on a pinnacle of the temple, And saith unto him, If thou be the Son of God, cast thyself down: for it is written, He shall give his angels charge concerning thee: and in their hands they shall bear thee up, lest at any time thou dash thy foot against a stone."

Here was what Christ said in return: "It is written again, Thou shalt not tempt the Lord thy God."

Finally, there was an appeal to the lust of the eyes: "Again the devil taketh him up into an exceeding high mountain, and sheweth him all the kingdoms of the world, and the glory of them; and saith unto him, All these things will I give thee, if thou wilt fall down and worship me."

Jesus rebuked Satan by saying, "Get thee hence, Satan: for it is written, Thou shalt worship the Lord thy God, and him only shalt thou serve."

And the result of this confrontation between Christ and Satan: "Then the devil leaveth him, and, behold, angels came and ministered unto him."

JESUS HEALING THE LAME BEGGAR

THROUGH HIS DEMONS

Christ encountered quite a few individuals possessed of demons, according to those incidents actually covered in Scripture. There would be doubtless scores of others not depicted because their sheer number would have required, as John said, so many books "that even the world itself could not contain ... [all] ... that should be written." [John 21:25]

As we said earlier, demons are fallen angels and Satan as Lucifer was the highest archangel in heaven, but while such an angel him-

LUCIFER'S DOMINION

self, he is also the ruler of all the others who joined him in rebellion and he is the chief angel of darkness. He controls the other rebels, dominates them, manipulating them according to his own desires.

Christ encountered two demon-controlled individuals quite early in His ministry, according to Matthew: "And when he was come to the other side into the country of the Gergesenes, there met him two possessed with devils, coming out of the tombs, exceeding fierce, so that no man might pass by that way." (Matthew 8:28-32)

While the religious leaders of the day didn't acknowledge Jesus as the promised Messiah, the Son of God, the demons did so immediately: "And, behold, they cried out, saying, What have we to do with thee, Jesus, thou Son of God? art thou come hither to torment us before the time?"

Jesus' exorcism resulted in quite a spectacular event: "And there was a good way off from them an herd of many swine feeding. So the devils besought him, saying. If thou cast us out, suffer us to go away into the herd of swine. And he said unto them, Go. And when they were come out, they went into the herd of swine: and, behold, the whole herd of swine ran violently down a steep place into the sea, and perished in the waters."

We also read: "And one of the multitude answered and said, Master, I have brought unto thee my son, which hath a dumb spirit; And wheresoever he taken him, he teareth him: and he foameth, and gnasheth with his teeth, and pineth away: and I spake to thy disciples that they should cast him out; and they could not. He answereth him, and saith, O faithless generation, how long shall I be with you? ... bring him unto me. And they brought him unto him: and when he saw him, straightway the spirit tare him; and he fell on the ground, and wallowed foaming. And he asked his father, How long is it ago since this came unto him? And he said, Of a child. And ofttimes it hath cast him into the fire, and into the waters, to destroy him: but if thou canst do any thing, have compassion on us, and help us. Jesus said unto him, If thou canst believe, all things are possible to him that believeth ... He rebuked the foul spirit, saying unto him, Thou dumb and deaf spirit, I charge thee, come out of him, and enter no more into him. And the spirit cried, and rent him sore, and came out of him: and he was as one dead; insomuch that many said, He is dead. But Jesus took him by the hand, and lifted him up; and he arose." (Mark 9:17-27) "And devils also came out of many, crying out, and saying, Thou art Christ the Son of God. And he rebuking them suffered them not to speak: for they knew that he was Christ." (Luke 4:41).

THE VISION OF DEATH

Manifestations in the World

CHAPTER VII:

No age has offered more eloquent testimony to the influence and work of Satan than that in which we live today. His purpose is being manifested through growing interest in Satanism, demonology, witchcraft, astrology, tarot card reading and other forms of occult endeavor.

OUR PRESENT REALITY

There can be little doubt that these situations fulfill prediction in the Bible. Here is what noted occult author Peter Haining wrote in *Witchcraft and Black Magic:* "I know from personal experience that witchcraft is flourishing in the United States. Young people in particular are very eager to join the numerous covens which can be found from New York to Los Angeles and Detroit to New Orleans. According to one authority, there is a flourishing coven in Hollywood, led by a former movie actress, and in Boston there are no fewer than thirteen. In Los Angeles the authorities have shown what must amount to the most amazing public acceptance of witchcraft in all history—they have appointed a Mrs. Louise Huebner as Official County Witch ... "

Books concerning the occult are selling well, especially if these promote power through the zodiac or improving the sex life of the reader through special potions and ceremonies. Merrill Unger, in *Beyond the Crystal Ball,* states, "The decade of the seventies has been called the dawn of the occult era, the 'age of Aquarius.' A revival of interest in psychic phenomena is everywhere evident. People want to know the future. A sorrowing widow attends a seance, seeking to communicate with the spirit of her deceased husband. A distinguished churchman, rejecting Christian supernaturalism, turns to spiritualism to consult the spirit of his departed son ... A distraught wife, abandoned by her husband, seeks solace in the horoscope and the study of astrology ... the magical arts are being proudly paraded in theatre, movies, television, radio and in the literature of the day. Traditional 'Christian' society, as a result of large-scale departure from biblical Christianity, is opening the floodgates to an inundation of witchcraft, magic, sorcery, tarot card reading, seances, spiritism ... Never has the crystal ball been so highly polished and popular or the Bible been so neglected." Elsewhere in his book, Unger plainly states that all such activities "subscribe to Satan and evil spirits."

A HARMLESS FANTASY?

On the surface, all this might appear to be really quite harmless. As one observer noted, if people want to indulge their fantasies without harm to others, let them go right ahead. But God sees it differently.

Deuteronomy 32:16-22 gives us an object lesson of God's reaction to "harmless fantasies:" "They provoked him to jealousy with strange gods, with abominations provoked they him to anger. They sacrificed unto devils, not to God; to gods whom they knew not, to new gods that came newly up, whom your fathers feared not. Of the Rock that begat thee thou art unmindful, and hast forgotten God that formed thee. And when the Lord saw it, he abhorred them, because of the provoking of his sons, and of his daughters. And he said, I will hide my face from them, I will see what their end shall be: for they are a very froward generation, children in whom is no faith. They have moved me to jealousy with that which is not God; they have provoked me to anger with their vanities: and I will move them to jealousy with those which are not a people; I will provoke them to anger with a foolish nation. For a fire is kindled in mine anger, and shall burn unto the lowest hell, and shall consume the earth with her increase, and set on fire the foundations of the mountains.''

For people to say that witchcraft and such are harmless is an imagination of the thoughts of the heart that is evil in itself!

THE WORK OF DEMONS

Supposedly authentic case histories of demon possession have never been more plentiful than at present. And many are—strikingly enough—occurring in the United States, not just in some primitive countries!

But there is another, more obvious manifestation of Satan's work on earth.

Sin.

It is everywhere, indeed has been a part of the makeup of every human being who ever lived, but today the manifestations are much more out in the open, with all forms of immorality increasingly apparent.

Paul deals with this in the first chapter of Romans, "Wherefore God also gave them up to uncleanness through the lusts of their own hearts, to dishonour their own bodies between themselves... For this cause God gave them up unto vile affections: for even their women did change the natural use into that which is against nature: And likewise also the men, leaving the natural use of the woman, burned in their lust one toward another; men with men working that which is unseemly . . . God gave them over to a reprobate mind, to do those things which are not convenient; Being filled with all unrighteousness, fornication, wickedness, covetousness, maliciousness; full of envy, murder, debate, deceit, malignity; whisperers, Backbiters, haters of God, despiteful, proud, boasters, inventors of evil things, disobedient to parents . . . Who knowing the judgment of God, that they which commit such things are worthy of death,

not only do the same, but have pleasure in them that do them."
(Romans 1:24-32)

This one portion of Scripture puts into perspective all the protestations of the gay liberation movement, wife-swapping agreements, pornographic films and dirty books! I John 3:8 sums up sin in 33 words: "He that committeth sin is of the devil; for the devil sinneth from the beginning. For this purpose the Son of God was manifested, that he might destroy the works of the devil."

SIN AND SUFFERING

The misery we see about us today—starving multitudes, children orphaned by war, people maimed and dying—stems from man's propensity for giving in to his sin *nature*. In the Garden of Eden, before man succumbed to Satan's temptations, there was sinless perfection: Adam and Eve were in close communion with God; they walked with Him daily.

But then sin did enter into Eden, and from that place of communion, Adam and Eve were expelled; thus began the many, many centuries of history through which have been recorded a staggering degree of evil and resultant suffering typified by the fall of Rome and the Dark Ages. There are many periods which reveal a fascination with sin and corruption; surely these were equally as corrupt as this present age. True, such times were evil but they were limited because the known world was limited; at present, however, human beings are over much of the globe, and there are billions of them, whereas in previous ages there were at most millions.

RESPECTABLE EVIL

And how has man responded to the clear evidence of Satan's reality, to his manifestations of evil in the world, to persuasions and practices which produce more sin and suffering? The answer is as amazing as it is ominous. Satan has grown more popular and gained respectability!

Witchcraft, demonology and other occultish pursuits are today achieving an acceptance and a respectability that was previously never known.

It used to be that people ran in fear from Satan; but, today, he is embraced with passion: and in at least one instance (the Church of Wicca) the United States Government recognizes an organization of Satan's as tax-exempt right along with Christian and Jewish places of worship.

In San Francisco, the Church of Satan is doing a thriving business. And hundreds of newspapers and magazines carry astrology columns and/or articles of advice by various witches; and there is a great deal else that is clearly in defiance of God's Word and in submission to the Master Deceiver.

Truly a day of darkness—ruled by the unholy Prince of Darkness!

SATAN SMITTEN BY MICHAEL

Victory over Satan

CHAPTER VIII:

Satan is engaged in warfare against not only God but also His creations, individual men and women who either know God and His Son in a redemptive way or who do not know God and are acting in a rebellious, deliberately sinful fashion.

How can any mortal, possessed of a sin nature and the fallibility of being human, hope to combat Satan, to hold him off, as it were, let alone gain complete victory over him?

Part of the answer lies in that Satan cannot change the eternal destiny or security of believers. He can make life for them here on earth as miserable as possible; and he can do everything in his power to keep unbelievers isolated from any real chance of salvation.

But we need only turn to the Bible for verse after verse telling us not only how to cope with Satan but how to gain both victory over Satan on earth and for eternity. James 4:7 gives us a simple rule: "Submit yourselves therefore to God. Resist the devil, and he will flee from you". And in II Corinthians 2:11 "Lest Satan should get an advantage of us: for we are not ignorant of his devices".

We read earlier how Jesus triumphed over Satan during a series of temptations. And in Mark 16:15-17 Jesus charged His disciples to follow His example. "And he said unto them, Go ye into all the world, and preach the gospel to every creature. He that believeth and is baptized shall be saved; but he that believeth not shall be damned. And these signs shall follow them that believe; In my name shall they cast out devils; they shall speak with new tongues".

Evidence of their success is given in Luke 10:17, "And the seventy returned again with joy, saying, Lord, even the devils are subject unto us through thy name". Again in Luke 9:1-2, "Then he called his twelve disciples together, and gave them power and authority over all devils, and to cure diseases. And he sent them to preach the kingdom of God, and to heal the sick."

GOD'S PLAN FOR THE BELIEVER

Victory ...

That's the word that should be foremost in the vocabulary of every true believer. It's a word that God gives and is implicit in the death, burial and resurrection of Jesus Christ, His Holy Son. Only in Christ is there victory and with Christ life can indeed be a series of triumphs over the adversary.

Probably the definitive portion of Scripture pertinent to this warfare can be found in the sixth chapter of Ephesians, verses 11 through 18: "Put on the whole armour of God, that ye may be able to stand against the wiles of the devil."

What is this "whole armour of God"?

In II Corinthians 6:7 we find the answer: "By the word of truth, by the power of God, by the armour of righteous ... " Righteousness is that armour. God exhorts us to lead righteous lives; some people think this means perfect lives and they look at believers around them and say, "They're far from perfect!" But righteousness is rather a striving toward lives ordered by God, a desire to be led by Him, to obey Him, to do that which pleases Him; no human being this side of heaven will be perfect but every believer can be righteous. And it is righteousness that is a first line of defense against the accuser.

THE SECOND STEP

Next, in Ephesians 6:14, we read, "Stand therefore, having your loins girt about with truth, and having on the breastplate of righteousness."

THE NEW JERUSALEM

In warfare the breastplate covered the lungs and the heart; so it should be in the spiritual warfare with Satan as the enemy.

But there is also a new word of advice—"your loins girt about with truth." God is not here speaking of loins in a physical sense. How do we know this? Because I Peter 1:13 says so: "Wherefore gird up the loins of your mind, be sober, and hope to the end for the grace that is to be brought unto you at the revelation of Jesus Christ."

We are to keep our minds pure and undefiled but, also, guarded and protected "with truth." What is this truth? That which is revealed in God's Word, namely, His redemptive plan and the implementation of that plan through His Son, Jesus Christ.

STILL MORE IS REQUIRED

"And your feet shod with the preparation of the gospel of peace." (Ephesians 6:15) According to Colossians 3:23-24, this is but simply: "Whatsoever ye do, do it heartily, as to the Lord, and not unto men; Knowing that of the Lord ye shall receive the reward of the inheritance: for ye serve the Lord Christ."

This is the gospel of peace, the peace of salvation through Christ; and we are constantly to be preparing ourselves for Him, this preparation yet another facet in victory over Satan.

Perhaps the most important facet, however, is emphasized by the words "above all," in Ephesians 6:16 "Above all, taking the shield of faith, wherewith ye shall be able to quench all the fiery darts of the wicked".

This is truly a pivotal verse. It says that we can defend ourselves against all Satanic attacks, not just some or most but every attack that Satan and/or his demons would mount against us is doomed to failure if we but put up that shield of faith, holding it proudly and confidently in front of us.

The last "piece" of defensive armour offered to us by St. Paul is the "helmet of salvation" in Ephesians 6:17. Salvation is the head of the body, so to speak; without it, the body would die, and here we are not speaking strictly of physical death but of another death, that which is referred to in the original Greek as "separation from God," or spiritual death. If we hold out the shield of faith, if we believe that God sent His Son to die on the Cross for our sins, and accept this into our lives, embracing to us all the attendant truths, Satan will not be able to strike any mortal blows; and with the helmet of salvation we have protected ourselves from him in this life and for all eternity.

THE WORD OF GOD

Then Paul gives us the one real piece of offensive equipment in this "arsenal." The latter part of verse 17 speaks of "the sword of the Spirit," and adds in explanation, that this is the "word of God." (Ephesians 6:17)

The powerful nature of the word of God is proven by Hebrews 4:12: "For the word of God is quick, and powerful, and sharper than any twoedged sword, piercing even to the dividing asunder of soul and spirit, and of the joints and marrow, and is a discerner of the thoughts and intents of the heart."

The Word is capable of doing all of this; there are no limitations:

God is all-powerful and so is His Word. Satan is but a pauper in the long run when compared to what God has to offer.

And as a final admonition, Paul states, "Praying always with all prayer and supplication in the Spirit, and watching thereunto with all perseverance and supplication for all saints." (Ephesians 6:18)

Prayer is a cornerstone of life in Christ; it is as water to a plant—neither the life nor the plant can remain healthy without nourishment. And prayer for the believer is spiritual nourishment. It links people to God, and allows them to communicate with Him, allows them to tell Him of their needs but, most importantly, to thank Him for the blessings given by Him. Prayer should include adoration, commitment and supplication.

BEFORE ALL ELSE

Thus, it is possible to gain victory over Satan, to keep him from achieving dominance in our lives. But there must be a beginning, you say; and then, you ask, "What is the first step?"

John 3:16 provides the answer: "For God so loved the world, that he gave his only begotten Son, that whosoever believeth in him should not perish, but have everlasting life."

THE MOUTH OF HELL

Satan's Destiny

CHAPTER IX

Satan's destiny is to fail. Of this the Bible leaves no doubt.

First, he is a conquered enemy, "Now is the judgment of this world: now shall the prince of this world be cast out." [John 12:31] Another indicative verse is the latter part of 1 John 3:8: "For this purpose the Son of God was manifested, that he might destroy the works of the devil."

Next, he is under a perpetual curse. As Genesis 3:14 states, "And the Lord God said unto the serpent, Because thou hast done this, thou art cursed above all cattle, and above every beast of the field; upon thy belly shalt thou go, and dust shalt thou eat all the days of thy life."

Isaiah 65:25 underlines this: "The wolf and the lamb shall feed together, and the lion shall eat straw like the bullock: and dust shall be the serpent's meat."

Further, Satan's destiny is to be punished. Not for a season, not for an extended period, but for eternity.

GOD'S JUSTICE

The Bible tells us there will be a time in the future of this world when Satan will be bound by God and held prisoner for a thousand years. Though the Book of Revelation is not history, but prophesy, the Bible often speaks in symbolic terms. For example, II Peter 3:8 tells us, "But, beloved, be not ignorant of this one thing, That one day is with the Lord as a thousand years, and a thousand years as one day." In Chapter 20:1-3, we read:

"And I saw an angel come down from heaven, having the key of the bottomless pit and a great chain in his hand. And he laid hold on the dragon, that old serpent, which is the Devil, and Satan, and bound him a thousand years. And cast him into the bottomless pit, and shut him up, and set a seal upon him, that he should deceive the nations no more, till the thousand years should be fulfilled: and after that he must be loosed a little season."

Following this event or, rather, during it, we have what is referred to as the millennial age.

THE END OF THE AGE

The end of the millennial age is to be characterized by apostasy and rebellion. As Revelation 20:7-9 points out, "And when the thousand years are expired, Satan shall be loosed out of his prison, And shall go out to deceive the nations which are in the four quarters of the earth, Gog and Magog, to gather them together to battle: the number of whom is as the sand of the sea.

Then the final battle of all time will take place, with Satan's army being dealt an eternal death blow. Why will he be unleashed? What is God's purpose for doing this? Dr. Unger writes, "The purpose of his loosing, in God's program, is that the archrebel might test man's loyalty to God during the last of God's ordered ages in time, before the dawn of eternity.

THE END OF THE PRINCE OF DARKNESS

The Lord Himself gave a clue in Matthew 25:41: "Depart from me, ye cursed, into everlasting fire, prepared for the devil and his angels."

To find an amplification of this, we simply turn to Revelation 20:10: "And the devil that deceived them was cast into the lake of fire and brimstone, where the beast and the false prophet are, and shall be tormented day and night for ever and ever."

This lake of fire and brimstone will be "occupied" first by Satan and his demons but, soon, they will be joined by others: "And I saw a great white throne, and him that sat on it, from whose face the earth and the heaven fled away; and there was found no place for them. And I saw the dead, small and great, stand before God; and the books were opened: and another book was opened, which is the book of life: and the dead were judged out of those things which were written in the books, according to their works. And the sea gave up the dead which were in it; and death and hell delivered up the dead which were in them: and they were judged every man according to their works. And death and hell were cast into the lake of fire. This is the second death. And whosoever was not found written in the book of life was cast into the lake of fire." [Revelation 20:11-15]

THE LAKE OF FIRE

THE KINGDOM ESTABLISHED

The new heaven and the new earth then ushered in will be everything that believers down through the centuries have hoped. "And God shall wipe away all tears from their eyes; and there shall be no more death, neither sorrow, nor crying, neither shall there be any more pain: for the former things are passed away." (Revelation 21:4)

In other ways, too, it will be a beautiful world: "And he shewed me a pure river of water of life, clear as crystal, proceeding out of the throne of God and of the Lamb. In the midst of the street of it, and on either side of the river, was there the tree of life, which bare twelve manner of fruits, and yielded her fruit every month: and the leaves of the tree were for the healing of the nations ... And there shall be no night there; and they need no candle, neither light of the sun; for the Lord God giveth them light: and they shall reign forever and ever." [Revelation 22:1-2,5]

AND FINALLY—

Even though Satan—the instigator of sin from the Garden of Eden through to Judgment Day—is on the loose today, will be tomorrow and for years to come, God will write the last chapter in his unholy story. Isaiah 14:12-19 tells us how it will read. "How are thou fallen from heaven, O Lucifer, son of the morning! how art thou cut down to the ground, which didst weaken the nations! For thou hast said in thine heart, I will ascend into heaven, I will exalt my throne above the stars of God: I will sit also upon the mount of the congregation, in the sides of the north: I will ascend above the heights of the clouds: I will be like the most High. Yet thou shalt be brought down to hell, to the sides of the pit. They that see thee shall narrowly look upon thee, and consider thee, saying, Is this the man that made the earth to tremble, that did shake kingdoms; That made the world as a wilderness, and destroyed the cities thereof; that opened not the house of his prisoners? All the kings of the nations, even all of them, lie in glory, every one in his own house. But thou art cast out of thy grave like an abominable branch, and as the raiment of those that are slain, thrust through with a sword, that go down to the stones of the pit; as a carcase trodden under feet."

In the meantime, God speaks reassuringly to us in John 14:27 through the words of his Son, Jesus Christ. "Peace I leave with you, my peace I give unto you: not as the world giveth, give I unto you. Let not your heart be troubled, neither let it be afraid."

VISION OF THE EMPYREAN

The Engravings of Gustav Doré, like many other works of art, present interpretive concepts which are often allegorical in nature. The manuscript has been developed from Scripture ... as given in the Bible.

Neither the art used for illustrations nor references in the manuscript are intended to make representations in conflict with doctrinal views or any Christian teachings.

CREDITS

Page 32: Satan; Page 35: Woodcuts; Page 40: Lucifer's Dominion; from the Bettmann Archive.